Ships, Boats and Things that Float

Scoular Anderson

CONTENTS

CAMBRIDGE
UNIVERSITY PRESS

UCL
Institute of Education

Quicker by boat

Thousands of years ago, it was difficult to travel. The land was covered in trees, bushes and **swamps**.

It was easier for people to travel by water. The first boats were tree trunks with some of the wood dug out. They were called dug-outs.

Dug-outs were very heavy and were hard to carry. So, people started to make boats of animal skin. The boats were light and could be carried easily.

skins were stretched over a frame of thin branches.

kayak

coracle

Thin but strong

Reeds are plants that grow in wet places. They are very light and thin, but if they are cut and tied together in bundles, they become strong. These bundles can be made into boats.

The Ancient Egyptians made quite big boats out of reeds called papyrus.

Bamboo is very flexible. It can be bent into shapes to make a boat.

← an Indian parisal

Thin strips of wood can be nailed together to make light boats. These are called clinker-built boats.

Oars for rowing

Rowing with **oars** is a good way to move a boat. Roman warships had two or even three rows of oars. The ships moved quickly with around one hundred men rowing.

A beak at the front was used to **ram** enemy ships.

Viking ships had a sail, but most of the time they were rowed. The ships had flat bottoms. They could move up **shallow** rivers or be pulled up on a beach.

Wind and sail

Before engines were invented, wind was used to move boats. You needed sails to catch the wind. Sails were made of **canvas** and were all shapes and sizes.

Dhows have triangular sails. They travel around the Indian ocean.

Christopher Columbus and his **crew** sailed across the Atlantic Ocean. His ship looked like this.

Most sailing boats were used to carry things from place to place. Small boats kept close to the land. Bigger boats were called ships. They could travel long distances.

8

Clippers were the fastest of all sailing ships.

The hull is the name of the main part of a boat. Outrigger boats have an extra, smaller hull. This helps keep the boat upright.

Hawaiian outrigger canoe →

hull

Some sailing ships were fighting ships. Frigates were big warships made of wood. They were fast and powerful and could change direction quickly. They had fifteen to twenty **cannons** on each side.

yards- sails were attached to these

The quarterdeck- the captain stood here to give orders.

stern (rear)

The ships wheel moved the rudder to steer the ship.

rudder

Gunports- the cannons fired out of these

Gunport lids were closed in stormy weather.

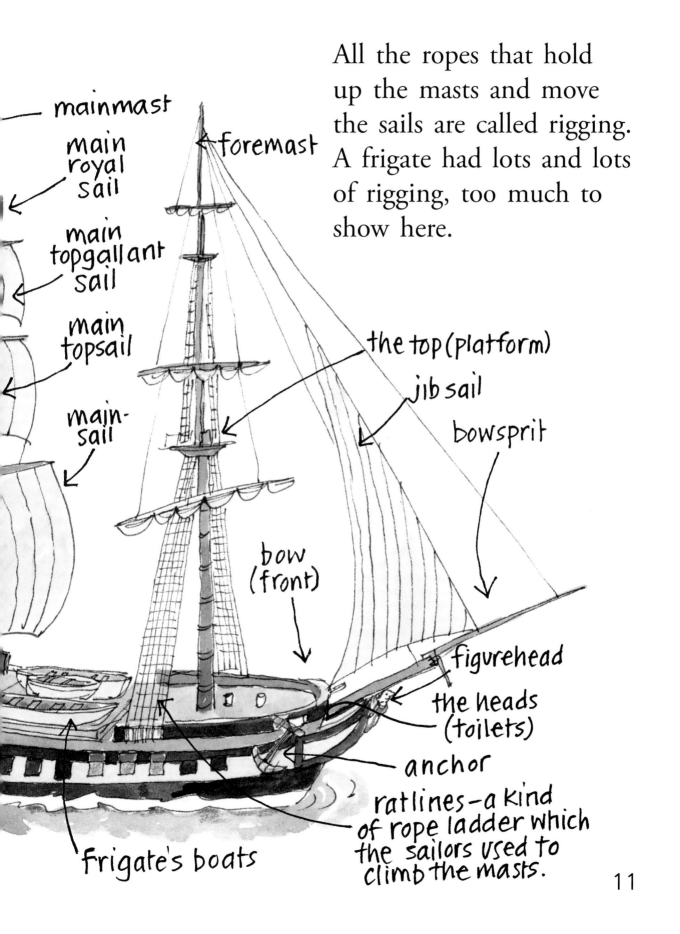

mainmast

main royal sail

main topgallant sail

main topsail

main-sail

foremast

All the ropes that hold up the masts and move the sails are called rigging. A frigate had lots and lots of rigging, too much to show here.

the top (platform)

jib sail

bowsprit

bow (front)

figurehead

the heads (toilets)

anchor

ratlines—a kind of rope ladder which the sailors used to climb the masts.

Frigate's boats

11

Full steam ahead!

If there was no wind, boats with sails couldn't move. The problem was solved when **steam engines** were invented. The first ships with engines were paddle steamers. They had paddles at each side or at the back.

paddles

Paddle wheelers were used on shallow rivers and lakes.

The Comet was one of the first ships to carry **passengers**. It still had sails in case the engine broke down!

About 150 years ago, ships became much bigger.
They were built of iron instead of wood.
They were driven by propellers at the back rather
than paddles.

the Great Britain's
propeller

The Great Britain was
built 170 years ago.
She carried passengers
across the Atlantic
Ocean with speed and
comfort.

Modern passenger **cruise liners** are enormous compared to the Great Britain. They are like floating towns with everything you want on a long journey. Nowadays ships are driven by **diesel** engines.

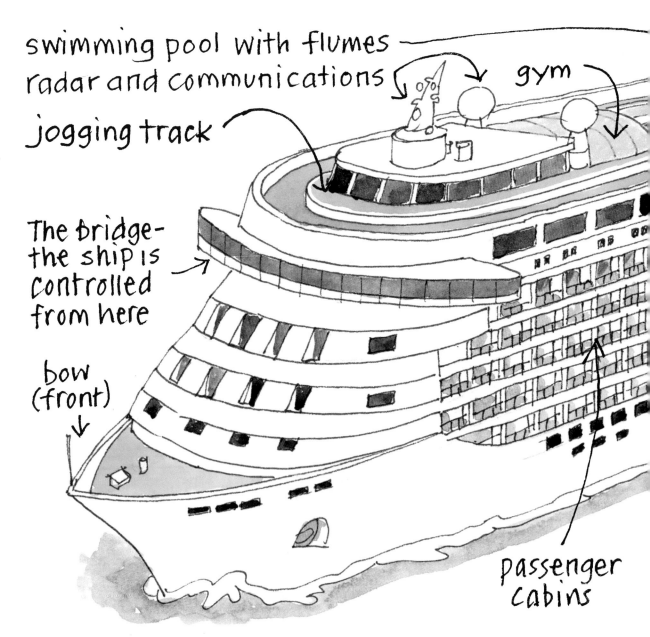

swimming pool with flumes

radar and communications

gym

jogging track

The bridge– the ship is controlled from here

bow (front)

passenger cabins

The biggest cruise ships can carry about 3,000 passengers and around 1,000 crew.

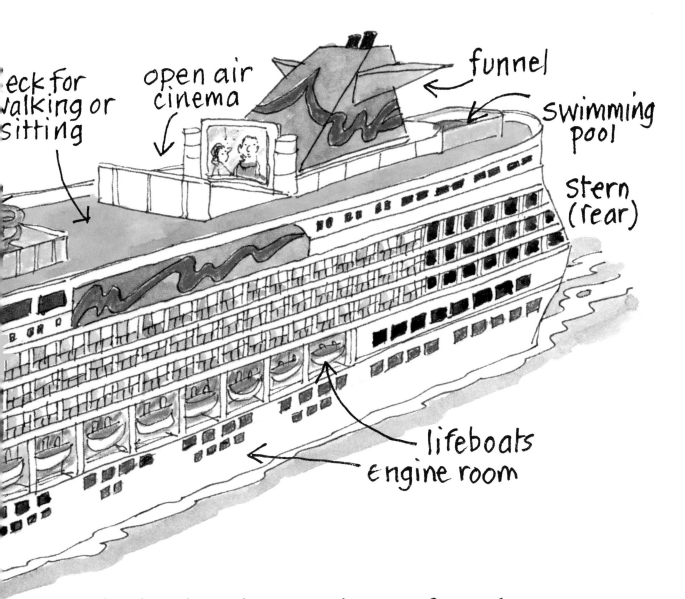

deck for walking or sitting

open air cinema

funnel

swimming pool

stern (rear)

lifeboats

engine room

Inside the ship there are bars, cafes and restaurants. There are shops, dance halls and a theatre. For young people there are computer games arcades and play areas.

Cargo

Nowadays, most big ships are used for carrying cargo. Cargo can be anything – food or glass, TV sets or shoes. The biggest ships sail to ports right around the world. Smaller cargo ships do shorter journeys. Container ships carry cargo packed into huge steel boxes.

Containers are stacked high on the container ship's deck.

Any cargo that is not in a container is called bulk. Bulk carriers carry things like oil, grain, coal or cement.

This ship carries gas.

A small ship is loading up with wood.

Some oil tankers are enormous.

Fun on the water

Moving about on the water can be fun for anyone. There are all sorts of ways that people can enjoy themselves on boats and things that float.

You can do all sorts of things with a board on water.

← a sailboard

a board pulled by a speedboat

a surfboard

RIBs are often used for search and rescue.

A jet ski is driven by a strong jet of water.

Small boats moved by oars or wind are called dinghies.

A pedalo is your own little paddle boat.

All sorts of ships

Nowadays, ships are built for all sorts of tasks.

An icebreaker smashes a path for other ships through frozen sea.

Oil rig ships drill for oil at the bottom of the sea.

Submarines travel mostly under water.

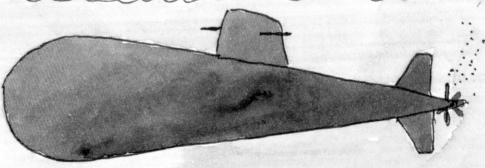

Hovercraft and airboats are driven along by huge fans. Both can travel on very shallow water.

Tugs are small but powerful. They help big ships to move around in ports.

There are even ships that carry ships.

Submersibles carry people deep down into the ocean.

GLOSSARY

cannons	guns which use gunpowder to fire cannonballs
canvas	very strong woven cloth
crew	people who work on a ship
cruise liners	passenger ships used for pleasure trips
diesel	kind of fuel
oars	long poles with a wider flat end used for rowing
passengers	travellers on a ship
ram	hit another boat on purpose
RIBs	rigid inflatable boats, which are powerboats fitted with a tube filled with air
shallow	something, such as water, that is not deep
steam engines	engines powered by steam
swamps	very wet, soft land, usually with lots of trees

INDEX

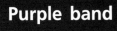
Ships, Boats and Things That Float — Scoular Anderson

Teaching notes written by Sue Bodman and Glen Franklin

Using this book

Developing reading comprehension

This brightly coloured, illustrated text explores the development of travel by water. It is a companion text to Sticks, Bricks and Bits of Stone (White band) which comes later in the Cambridge Reading Adventures. Non-fiction features, such as labels and captions, are used in an entertaining way to add meaning and support comprehension.

Grammar and sentence structure

- Sentences incorporate a range of connectives to develop ideas over two or more clauses.
- Verb usage is more advanced, including use of conditional verbs.

Word meaning and spelling

- Subject-specific words, supported by glossary and labelling.
- Longer, multi-syllabic words ('container', 'nowadays') requiring attention to word detail.

Curriculum links

Geography – not all children live in regions served by the sea. Topics could explore modes of transport in land-locked countries.

History – use this book in conjunction with other non-fiction texts to investigate the development of transport and travel, or if studying specific periods of history such as the ancient Egyptians.

Learning outcomes

Children can:

- recognise how words are used to literary effect to achieve authorial purpose
- adapt to the different styles employed in the text
- take note of punctuation and use it to keep track of longer sentences
- solve most unfamiliar words using appropriate word-reading strategies, and monitor that meaning is gained.

A guided reading lesson

Book Introduction

Give each child a copy of the book. Ask them to read the front cover and the blurb. Then ask them to quickly flick through and tell you what type of book they think this is: it is a non-fiction text, but looks different to many information books children may be familiar with.

Orientation

Turn to the title page and skim the contents. Ask: *Does this help us to decide what type of book we are going to be reading today?* Remind children of the purposes for reading non-fiction, i.e. to find specific information related to topics of interest. Say: *In this book, we can find out lots of interesting facts about how people learned to travel around the world in boats and ships.* For children who have no experience of the sea, some photographs or short video clips could help to set the scene.

Preparation

Page 2: Look at the heading '*Quicker by boat*'. Ensure that children understand this more literary use of language.

Ask the children to read pages 2 and 3 quietly and then explain what the author means by his heading.

Pages 8 and 9: Look at the different ways the main text and the captions are presented. Read the caption about Columbus. Ask: *Why is this information given in a caption?* Discuss how it provides more specific information to supplement the main text on this page. Look at the word '*crew*' on this page. Check children know why this is in bold. Ask: *What do you think this word means? Read the caption and tell me what you think. Now turn to the glossary. Is this what you thought?*

Page 14: Use this page to explore the use of captions and labels. How are they different? Look at how they are used to explore the features of the ship.